Verses From Above

Praise the Lord!
      On Man and Nature
            Garden of Abuse

Judy A. Dees

authorHOUSE®

AuthorHouse™
1663 Liberty Drive, Suite 200
Bloomington, IN 47403
www.authorhouse.com
Phone: 1-800-839-8640

© 2008 Judy A. Dees All Rights Reserved

No part of this book may be reproduced, stored in a retrieval system, or transmitted by any means without the written permission of the author.

First published by AuthorHouse November 18, 2008

ISBN: 978-1-4389-1617-0 (sc)
ISBN: 978-1-4389-1616-3 (dj)

Library of Congress Control Number 2008909501

Printed in the United States of America
Bloomington, Indiana

This book is printed on acid-free paper.

TABLE OF CONTENTS

PREFACE xi
DEDICATION xv
ACKNOWLEDGEMENTS xvii

PRAISE THE LORD!

PRAISE THE LORD! 1

Lost Then Found 3

SLEEPY SUBMISSION 5
NO GOING BACK 6
YOU REACHED OUT 7
I CAN DREAM OF HEAVEN 8
THE CITY SLEEPS 9
NO FEAR 10

Trials or Afflictions Follow 11

VALLEY OF MY LORD 13
ALL THINGS 15
CASUALTY OF WAR 16
THE LOOK IN YOUR EYES 17
THROUGH? 18
ONE MORE DAY 20
IT ALL PASSED BY ME 21
DON'T GIVE UP 23

Lukewarmness Resulted 25

REEL ME IN 27

TEPID TOES 29
PICKLED? 30
THE LIVING DEAD 32
LACK FROM ABOVE 33
SPIRALING BRANCH, HOLY SPIRIT VINE 34
DO I DARE ? 35

God Is in Control 37

YOURS TO ORDER 39
TAKE MY HAND 40
I COULD NOT SEE 42
SOMETIMES 43
A TO Z PRAYER 44
RUNNING FROM YOUR PLAN 45

God Shows Love and Protection 47

SWEET HONEY 49
LIKE AN UNLOVED CHILD 50
WHAT IS THAT TO ME ? 52
CLAIM THOSE PROMISES! 53
GLORY OF THE LORD 54
BIG! 55
FIRE GUIDE 57

Receive His Spirit's Fruit 59

FRUIT OF THE SPIRIT 61
PEACE BE STILL 62
THE RIVER 63

Just Praise the Lord! 65

LIFTED TO YOU 67
YOU AND ME, FATHER 68
I SAY I CANNOT SEE YOU 69
I LOOK BACK 70
WHATEVER 71
I LOVE YOU! 72

ON MAN AND NATURE

ON MAN AND NATURE 75
FIFTY YEARS LATER 77
IN THE COMPANY OF UGLINESS 79
TUMBLEWEED BLUES 80
BARREN FIELDS OF THE HEART 81
WEB OF DECEIT 82
DELAYED DECAY 83
FROM A BUTTERFLY TO A COCOON 85
FLOWER OF SOCIETY 86
PRAIRIE MAN OF OLD 87
SHARED WITH HIS CREATION 89
TUMBLEWEED LIFE 90
AFTERNOON MOUNTAIN SHOWER 91
MR. MOON 92
SNOW BEAUTY 93
SNOW 94
DREAMER'S FEAST 95
LITTLE SNOWFLAKE 96

SON - GLOW RADIANCE 97
BIRD OF FAITH 98
I AM THE WORM 99
KNOW 100
PRAIRIE HUMMMMM 101
CONFETTI ENCHANTMENT 102
SUNFLOWER GIRL 103
REAP OF INNOCENCE 104
SILENT LASS 106
FADED DREAMS 107
POETIC COLLAGE 109
PRAIRIE GROVE 110
PRAIRIE MAIDEN 112
THRESHING TIME 114
VIBRANT DEMISE 115

GARDEN OF ABUSE

GARDEN OF ABUSE 117
GARDEN OF ABUSE 120
BETRAYAL 122
FETAL PAYMENT PLAN 124
PROSTITUTED INNOCENCE 126
SPOONFED IMAGINATION 127
I NEVER KNEW 129
BLESSED EXCHANGE 131
WALLS 132
FROM ONE WHO HURTS 134

CHILD OF ABUSE 135
REJECTION 136
SPIRIT OF FEAR 137
TANGLED 138
INNOCENT GLEE 139
DADDY, DADDY 141
O, LITTLE CHILD 142
PAST CORRIDOR HALLS 144
DARKNESS POUNDING 146
REMINISCING 147
LIFTED 148
SON-FILLED RADIANCE 150
WHAT THE LOCUSTS HAD TAKEN 151
A MOTHER'S HAND 153
WHERE DO I BEGIN ? 155
ONCE ENSLAVED 157
IT BROKE MY HEART 158
FAKE ONE 161
SOFT, SPLENDOR MOMENT 163
DARE TO BE 164
IT'S TIME 165
VISIT BRANSON, MISSOURI 167

PREFACE

As its name *VERSES FROM ABOVE* implies, this book of poetry is from the Lord. Now, I want to share with you the gift He gave me. Although an English teacher of twenty-five years and an avid student of the English language, I had never been able to actually write poetry; teaching and encouraging it were all I could do. The poems in this book came during a long period in which I was ill and virtually housebound. I was finally quiet and still before the Lord, and the poetry began to flow.

These poems are for anyone and everyone. Each person was created by God; each can identify with nature in some respect; and each has been abused in some manner - or knows others who have been. I pray the poems speak to you in the way He intends. Any less than acceptable poetry in this book must be from my pen; any that are acceptable and speak to your spirit are surely from His pen.

A few of these poems contain words that do not exist in Webster's dictionaries; a few use an incorrect form of the word written; and some have sentence structure that is unusual or somewhat incorrect. However, I did not dare change the words given me except for basic editing.

PRAISE THE LORD! **Addresses our marvelous Lord - God the Father, God the Son, and God the Holy Spirit - and His roles and deeds in a person's life.** At age thirty-nine, I met Him on my bathroom floor, and for the past twenty plus years, my life has not been the same. I was saved that night in the presence of only God and me. Later, I officially accepted Jesus as my Savior and Lord.

ON MAN AND NATURE **explores the similarities between mankind and the elements of nature.** We are both live entities, and, as such, perhaps have a few things in common. Although I often seem like a lion or a butterfly, I see myself as a flower (once a "Flower of Society" and a "Prairie Maiden"). With which part of nature can you most identify?

GARDEN OF ABUSE **was the chapter I withheld most; it is very personal - for me and for the images of people locked in my mind.** Abuse is so ugly. How may a garden come from it? It can, and it does! Some of the most beautiful people I have met or known are the unique, colorful beauties in my world. What happens to each person definitely shapes his or her personality, values, and choices - every facet of life. As in a garden, one can dig out the thorns, weeds, and rocks, thus having good soil in which to flourish, OR one can allow the thorns, weeds, and rocks to flourish, thus leaving an ugly wasteland.

The pages of this book lay dormant ("Delayed Decay") for over fifteen years. They were tucked away in cabinets, boxes, notebooks, and sacks. Near the same time that a restlessness began growing inside me, the poems began re-appearing.

Several people kept mentioning the writing I had done, and I recalled that I had asked God to stir-up my gifts. I had also asked Him to show me my acres of diamonds and how to dig for them. Then, my younger daughter needed a part-time job, so the typing began - and this book evolved.

DEDICATION

To the One who knew me before I was born and yet chose my creation; the One who never ever left me in the worst times of my life; the One who gave me hope when I had no hope; the One who was my spiritual husband and best friend the many years I was alone; the One who is the Maker of Heaven and Earth; the One who walked with me through the valley of the shadow of death and saved my life; and the One who pulled me out of the mire and saved my soul: the One true Lord God Almighty, the real author of this book. Thank you, Lord! I love you!

I also know there are two more dedications that need mention (1) The loves of my life on earth, my daughters Tricia Tice DeWitt and Tara Tice Fleming. You have been with me all your lives, much of mine. You know me most intimately and walked much of my path with me, often to your disadvantage. (2) My precious former students in Huntsville, Harrison, and Mt. Judea, AR (Judy Tice Dees); Lavaca, AR (Judy Benham); and Fairbanks, AK (Judy Dees); and my oldest grandchild Cole DeWitt, whom I home schooled. All of you, in being so important to me, are woven into the tapestry of my life. I think I learned as much (if not more) from my children, grandchild, and students as they learned from me.

ACKNOWLEDGEMENTS

People help people make it through life. There are times, however, when extra help is needed. For people in good times and bad, we need to be most grateful. I thank God for the wonderful people He chose to put in my life - past, present, and future. They are too numerous to mention. I do want to give special thanks to some who helped me the past few difficult years in which I was virtually housebound (being still enough for this book to come, thus your help in bringing it to print):

My husband Randy who has loved me when I needed it most and who stayed beside me in my years of near confinement; my friends Kathy Cox and Lucy Slater who kept calling when I didn't want to talk with anyone, thus helping me "hold on for dear life"; our friends and neighbors Rodney and Karen Keys who invited us to their house for events and requested that all guests come fragrance - free for my safety; Dr. Cathy Clary who provided not only excellent health care but also a caring ear and heart; Dr. Aubrey Worrell (deceased), Ted Stansbery, and Rick McLarty who walked me through natural healing; and my daughters and their husbands (Tricia and Chris DeWitt, Tara and Andrew Fleming) who made their homes chemical and fragrance free so I could visit them and be with my precious grandchildren

Cole, Cade, and Katie.

My spiritual help came from the Holy Spirit, assisted, for the most part, by Dave and Joyce Meyer Ministries, Charles Stanley's In Touch Ministries, Radio Bible Class, and Bobby & Lynn Crow's World Missions Outreach. I could not attend church because of the overwhelming fragrances there, so the teachings of and prayers of these ministries were an anchor for me. Thank you for loving the Lord and for being used by the Holy Spirit to minister to shut-ins like I was.

PRAISE THE LORD!

I lift up my eyes to the hills
Where does my help come from?
My help comes from the Lord,
The Maker of heaven and earth.
(Psalm 121: 1-2, NIV)

Lost Then Found

SLEEPY SUBMISSION

Laden with somniferous deference,
I began my journey to the throne;
"I must begin," is all I knew,
Gladly ignorant of its treacherous way.

Innocence allowed me, first, time to play.
Thoughts of hide-and-seek turned into a test;
Lost directions thrilled, then, later, chilled me.
Who knew the Devil was real, not a mean imposter?

Minutes, hours; then days and years,
Evil forces tried to surround, then defeat me.
"What armor of God? What prayer in the spirit?"
Oft thought I, when lost in one of many spiritual mazes.

Laden with somniferous deference,
I continue my journey to the throne;
"I must continue," is all I know,
Gladly knowledgeable of its treacherous way.

JAD: Salvation is, at first, a honeymoon with God. Then, "The honeymoon is over." Reality surfaces, and the war between good and evil becomes the Christian's daily spiritual occupation.

NO GOING BACK

I kept trying to go back
To the way things were,
Though tattered and torn
By Master's great hand;
He left nought any piece
Of my life untouched,
Yet I kept trying to gather
Scattered fragments from the ground.

"Don't you know my way is better?"
He asked this little child.
"Of course it must be, Father,"
Said I, more than a little rattled.
"Then stop trying to save
Old broken pieces
When you can have the new life
I, to you, impart.

With the old you will
Never again be content,
For my blood and life
Make all things new.
The old has passed;
Let it take flight to leave.
With eyes set fast on Me,
There will be no going back."

YOU REACHED OUT

Oh, Lord, You reached out
And saved me;
Oh, Lord, You reached out
And set me free;
When I called out to You on high,
You reserved my place
In Your sweet by and by.

From rusted chains
I thought to never be free,
But You, Oh God, came
So men might clearly see;
Blinded and tormented by evil legions,
No other cared to loose me
From inner entrapped regions.

You are the victor,
I, the thankful spoil.
From evil's grasping hand,
I am determined to recoil;
You reached out with Your loving hand,
Now I dance a joyful song
With mighty angels' band.

I CAN DREAM OF HEAVEN

Lord Jesus, You were spat upon,
Called names, and accused,
Rejected, scorned, beaten,
Dragged, and abused;
You left the splendor of Heaven
For this to endure?
Violations you forgave,
Salvation to secure.

No man could ever be
Greater than this,
And with You we be
In eternal bliss;
Your loving favor
I pray to receive;
Forgiveness divine,
No need to deceive.

Oh, to be more like You,
Will it ever be?
I am only human,
Imperfect as You can see.
Thank You, Jesus,
Your blood shed for my sins,
Now, I can dream of Heaven
Where life anew begins.

THE CITY SLEEPS

Shrouded mist cover lay
Over city sleeping,
Its inhabitants unaware
Of the deadly battle ensuing.
Angels versus demons,
Good opposing bad;
Which souls will fall prey
To the Evil One today?

Hurrying to and from
Daily appointed tasks,
Is human's way or God's way
The path they choose today?
Winds of dissension,
Toll of time fretted away;
Evil - lurking, listening,
Planning to use arrows without delay.

Dear Blind One,
Open your eyes before you fall.
Dear Deaf One,
Dare to listen, then you can hear.
Dear Lame One,
You must believe so you can walk.
Dear Hurting One,
Reach for His hand to pull you through.

Still, the city sleeps.

NO FEAR

No fear! Christ is near!
Belief so sweet avoids defeat;
Timeless drift given to thrift,
Savior God deserves great applaud.

No time to waste! Great need for haste!
Souls dying lost, consider such great cost;
Whom will you feed, for their lost soul plead?
Whom will you lead to Him who did bleed?

Neighbor next door? One who lies poor?
Prisoner behind bars,? An enemy who wars?
A child in your home? A foreigner in Rome?
Friends of your years? Hurt ones in tears?

No fear! Christ is near!
Who will draw apart, then from Him depart?
He never leaves, but for us he grieves.
Come to Him now, and lean on His vow.

Trials or Afflictions Follow

VALLEY OF MY LORD

Living on a mountain top brings comfort enough to me,
But my mountain top gets lonely, my sight set less on you.
Nowhere except in valleys can Your work on me be done,
So, Lord, leave me in the valley, if near You I will be.

My valley must be one of the endless kinds,
For daily I awaken to see my map charted thus.
"What valley today?" I ask my Lord.
"My Child, you have need of this one; we'll begin right away.

The civilized, winding valleys you've already passed by;
The ones you have remaining no other has seen or walked.
Each of these I've chosen especially for you
(For each of my creations, unique as they may be).

This valley will bring you chill and dread;
It is the Valley of the Shadow of Death.
My rod and my staff will have to comfort you,
For you'll not know where I am, as this course you tread.

It will leave you sick and trembling,
Thinking you are alone and lost;
But just know that I AM with you -
And will be - even when Death does by you pass."

Judy A. Dees

JAD: At age 39, I accepted Jesus as Savior. I put ALL I had on the altar of God. Next thing I knew, except for God and my husband, I lost all that was important to me - my two children, my students, my health, and my income. For several long years, I felt somewhat like I think Job must have felt. God worked and worked on me. No place except in this valley could His work on me be done. He was with me every step of the way; then healing and restoration began!

Verses From Above

ALL THINGS

"All things work together," says the Bible dear,
"For those who give God their love and fear."
Not SOME things but ALL things, I must recall,
When crying and clutching some dead-end wall.

Face-to-face combat with facets of doubt,
Nose-to-nose confrontation with sin's daily bout;
Cheek-to-cheek struggle of lonely desolation,
Back-to-back reoccurrence of fatigued isolation.

As a dreamer - dazed - and by pain's numbness driven,
When, out of catatonic state has striven,
Finds nothing changed in life's dreaded situation.
Can belief exist for promised Biblical proclamation?

Each struggle that does this one pursue,
Gnawing doubts hinder the mind to renew;
Consuming fears take their toll on searching thoughts.
God says He'll use them ALL, so why all the nervous knots?

JAD: Sleepless one night, I kept having this verse in Romans 8:28 roll through my mind. Finally, I had to get up, and with flashlight in hand, pen the burning sensation that was on my very fingertips. The next day, two of my Bible readings revolved around this same verse!

CASUALTY OF WAR

Sifted by the Devil himself,
Not even a trace of mercy or kindness;
Not once or twice but o'er and o'er,
Sifted, 'til nothing was left.

Dry as long desert stretches of road,
Deflated like a punctured, discarded balloon,
Stretched to a limit that merits no return,
Beaten - a vagrant left dead under roadside trash.

In a third of four stages of warrior preparation,
Blood-stained emotions unable to carry on and
Tear-filled existence unable to raise its head,
Where is my Father, Father of this casualty of war?

JAD: For years I sat in church. I never knew, however, until I was truly saved, that there is a DAILY war between good and evil, Satan and Christians. Sifted. Think on the meaning of that word.

THE LOOK IN YOUR EYES

I looked into Your face, Lord Dear,
Knowing now that this delight brought my demise;
As a moth so drawn to light's pleasure of death,
Mortal man cannot live after viewing Holy Grace.

That look of deep consternation I noticed in Your eyes:
Had I known its reason, could I have dared draw so near?
But innocent child to its parent will go,
You, Jesus, perfected parental Lamb of Woe.

I saw You again, as I walked from searing flames,
A look of relief offset by Your gentle smile;
You took my hand in Yours, as we laughed and skipped away,
The same hand that had shown me the way inside that fire!

JAD: In deep prayer to my Lord this day, I had no idea the long trial of illness I would be facing. Many times over thenext several years, I would think on this "vision." It helped me survive my long years of being virtually housebound.

Judy A. Dees

THROUGH?

Year after year
Of toilsome drear,
Making my nest
Became a daily test.
He took my babes
In differing shades,
Next went my job;
What had I left to rob?

I thought He had my all,
Until I heard His call,
"You've not everything given,
But you still are forgiven."
Ever failing health
Brought yearly fearful stealth;
For a woman nearing fifty,
I was now only a little bit nifty.

No work could I find
Brought peace to my frenzied mind
Or even a remote hidden bank account
Of any sizable amount;
Time to release the grasp
Of self-sufficiency's clasp,

So dropped my last reserve,
Fearful I'd receive what I deserve.

Verses From Above

Now You have all I own
Of life's earthly throne;
Besides spirit, body, and soul,
My loves and possessions in whole.
I stand before You -
Naked and bare - with no ado;
Either Your Word is true,
Or truly, I am through.

ONE MORE DAY

If You say no, that's okay;
I'm going to ask You anyway.
"Please heal me, Lord, and make me whole;
I hurt each day from the bottom of my soul.

Day after day, I pray its course has run,
But come the night, still quite undone;
My faith is waning; can I hold on?
To fight this fight, will strength be gone?

Hold on to me, Lord God up Above,
I'll sink and faint without Your dear love;
Through valleys and trenches have I trod,
Just one more day, Lord, help me plod."

JAD: MCS (multiple chemical sensitivities) affected me for ten or fifteen years before it consumed me. I had to quit my twenty-five year teaching profession, and for most of eight years, I was housebound. Day after day, I battled an enemy of which I had no knowledge. After three years of severe depression (and not able, thankfully, to take anti-depressants) and much prayer, I was able to see a faint light of hope. After five years of battling an enemy I finally understood, I exited my dark tunnel.

IT ALL PASSED BY ME

For long years,
The struggle was daily;
It seemed You
Had forgotten me, my Lord.
Cries rippled solitary
In darkest night's shrouded cover;
Sunlight could not penetrate
The murky ire of depression.

But You were there
Through it all,
With me every weary
Step of the way.
You held me up
When my feet were past walking;
You cuddled me when,
In exhausted faint, my soul reposed.

Then something happened!
Your gentle word was barely heard.
"I AM here, my Child;
It all passed by Me.
I allowed it all;
You've had no need to fear."
Slow peace, then
What joy filled my wasted soul!

Judy A. Dees

My Father, I come to You
On bended knee.
There is nothing left of me;
You took it all.
Christ living through me
Is all I desire;
Your presence, unknowingly,
The answer to my prayer.

DON'T GIVE UP

Dear Brother and Sister,
Don't give up!
I am now nearing
The other side of doom
And can tell you
It is worth all the pain.
My eyes have seen the glory
Of the comfort of the Lord.

When wasted soul thought
It was dying,
When heart-rending sob
Penetrated darkest night,
And when scattered emotions had lost
All semblance of sanity,
Hope's lost horizon awakened
In me a new dawn.

A soldier is not made
In the trenches;
Faith does not come
With sight;
Character beds not
Among the roses.
Christ Himself had to be
Crucified before He arose.

Judy A. Dees

Faint not, doubt not,
Despair not;
It is He who
Will pull you through.
Take one more step,
Breathe one more breath,
Knowing all is well
In Lord God's almighty hand.

Lukewarmness Resulted

REEL ME IN

Like a flopping fish on shore -
Neither in nor out -
Miserable I lay in hot, dry sun
Waiting for relief;
It never came, to my dismay,
As I lay so still.
"What to do, oh, my Lord,
You Fisherman of Men?"

"You'll never find peace or
My blessed relief," said He,
"When on your stomach,
Lying in between;
My kingdom is not One
For complacent compromise.
I died to show the depth of My love.
Was that not enough?

I called oft to you,
My eternal home to give;
It's not mere chance that
Left you stranded here.
I love you endless
Is all I will say.
Choose, like a fish,
To take out to sea."

Judy A. Dees

In the net of Your love
Is where I want to be,
Not floundering in
Some dark, dangerous deep;
So, Lord, reel me in -
This dry and dying fish.
In another day, I'll be gone.
Reel harder, Lord, for me!

Verses From Above

TEPID TOES

Tepid toes of humanity
Line the streets of Hell;
Wastlings walking to and fro,
Regretted choices mumbled into stagnant air.

"If I be not hot or I be not cold,
From His mouth I will be spewed."
I had not heard of tepid toes,
Until down its dangerous path I trod.

JAD: Even after I became aware of being hot-and-cold with the Lord, I found myself tepid on issues that required a hot or cold response. Hanging on to the familiar or desired often takes me into undesirable territory.

PICKLED?

Pickled ears, pickled eyes,
Pickled heart, pickled feet,
My Lord and God, give me more
Of your Word for meat!
I have no money,
I have no reputation,
Only a hungry soul
Ready for saturation.

As a cucumber soaks
In the early morning dew,
My heart and soul long
For more of You;
A storehouse of Word,
A reservoir of prayer,
Prepares me to be
Mighty Savior's warrior.

Waiting for vinegar cover
To work its transformation -
Healing trials and pains,
Beginning a reformation;
Seeing, hearing, feeling, walking -
All a fresh new start.
Only You, Lord can use the brine of life
To change my fickle heart.

Verses From Above

JAD: A girlfriend (Diane Mitchell) had a vision from God. All she saw was a big pickle! Her vision brought forth this poem. We think God was telling her to give Him her heart, eyes, head, and feet.

THE LIVING DEAD

I awaken to find myself among the living dead.
Where had I been? When did it all begin?
I had been sinking deep in sin's sand,
Unaware of how quickly it was sucking me in.

Deeper and deeper I sank in its mire,
Never for sure just what would transpire.
One moment missed with Lord Jesus Christ
Soon turned its passing timer to one lonely week.

A week without my morning daily bread
Soon rolled into a never ending month.
By then, my hunger abated, I was unaware;
Signs of deprivation missed my listless eyes.

I became one of them: living, but really dead.
A cistern not filled with living water
Soon sees stagnation and shallowness.
Life continues its drain; the pool, now dry.

JAD: Satan's tool of busyness is one way to assure neglect of the Word and prayer. Without water, the body becomes unhealthy and clogged; it can eventually die. Likewise, are the spirit and soul of a man who is deprived of the Living Water.

LACK FROM ABOVE

I've wandered so far
Off the railway of life,
Being so confused and shattered
By busyness and strife;
Where once there were footprints
In soft petals' flood,
Now, nothing but dried ruts
In crusted, earthy mud.

Father, I long to bask in the warmth
And beauty of Your love,
My hungry soul can no longer last
With this lack from Above;
For You fill me, Lord,
With an everlasting desire,
Strength give me to come Home,
Where I shall forever retire.

SPIRALING BRANCH, HOLY SPIRIT VINE

Jesus, blessed Savior,
To you I confess my sin,
I ask You, my Lord,
To pull me back in;
In Your loving arms
I surely belong,
But sin and shame try
To take love's song.

You are my redeemed,
And I am thine -
This spiraling branch
And Holy Spirit Vine;
Wash me and make me
Consecrated to You,
When life's murky mire
I have to walk through.

Hold me and make me
What You, Lord, desire,
Eyes up to Heaven,
My thoughts to aspire;
Dream days of earth's ways
I can't help but see,
The Son's face for the human race -
Free, free, free!

DO I DARE ?

Do I dare stand
Straight, tall, and firm,
When all around me is
Twisted, swayed corruption?
Do I dare lift
My eyes and arms to my Maker,
When all around me is
Self-centered, compromised apathy?

Do I dare sink
My roots into a deeper foundation,
When all around me is
Shallow, shifted sand?
Do I dare use
My fruit for right,
When all around me is
An orchard preserved?

I dare not go
The way of the wicked,
For who would pray
For them before our Righteous Judge?
I dare not take
A stand for wrong,
For who would know
The way to right?

Judy A. Dees

I dare not try to make
No difference in this world,
For who would know
The way out of life's forest?
I dare not worship
Any but the one true God,
For who would lead me
When my feet go astray?

God Is in Control

YOURS TO ORDER

Let my days be
Yours to order?
Let my own desires
Be nothing?
Father, when all my days
Are in such disorder,
How can I let them be
Yours to order?

Could it be the mess they're in
Results from my self-sufficiency sin?

How can I let
My desires be nothing?
They've never even been
A little of something.
If I put my all
In the palm of Your hand,
Will you save me
From life's sinking sand?

JAD: Try as we might to control our lives, the Lord is the One who directs our steps. Since the plans He has for us are for our good, why do we constantly try to inject our own?

TAKE MY HAND

Lord, take my hand,
For down the path I must tread,
I am now willing to go.

I may not be ready-
Only You can ascertain that -
But here I am; please take my hand.

I know You will have to
Lead me - perhaps drag me-
And carry me through.

Most assuredly I will be worn, weak, and
Weary - perhaps even faint-
Barely able to make it through.

I stood looking at my life:
The past, present, and future
That lay before me.

Suddenly, came realization that I
No longer controlled my life -
And had not for some time now.

I was bought at a precious price:
My life and sins, an exchange for One
Sacrificed on the Cross.

Verses From Above

Nothing I can do
Will alter the fate
You now have planned for me.

Trembling and weak,
I got off bended knees,
Wrinkled from fallen pool of tears.

Dried my fearful, swollen eyes
That, in terror,
Had been searching on the ground.

Cast them upward to Heaven's light,
Clear sight now granted
For mortal, earthly blindness.

"My Child, my Child! You finally found home.
I AM - and I know the plans I have for you.
Now you take MY hand!"

I COULD NOT SEE

I could not see the promises laid before me,
The Almighty's great hand stretched out wide;
I could not see the depth of His love for me,
Its radiance shining through darkest night.

I could not see the plans He had for me,
Love's light shining to make clear the way;
I could not see, for human eyes are blind
To spiritual mysteries seen only by Spirit's eyes.

I could not see that truly all works for my good;
Even in bad, He makes His way known.
I could not see, for I was blinded by sight;
Then the faith walk began, and in not seeing, I saw.

SOMETIMES

SOMETIMES
I walk beside the still waters,
SOMETIMES
I fly with the wings of an eagle;
SOMETIMES
I see lights of the Promised Land,
SOMETIMES
I envision glimpses of my Savior and Lord.

SOMETIMES
I have the valor of Daniel in the lion's den,
SOMETIMES
I possess the loyalty and patience of Job;
SOMETIMES
I use the wisdom of King Solomon,
SOMETIMES
I feel like David, a man after God's own heart.

SOMETIMES
I battle spiritually like Peter and Paul,
SOMETIMES
I believe with the faith of Father Abraham;
ALWAYS
I know He's changing me into a likeness of Him,
ALWAYS
I know I am His child, and he is my Father God.

Judy A. Dees

A TO Z PRAYER

In all the different ways I pray,
From when I rise 'til at night I lay,
On my heart are stories of old
Told about Your servants of gold.

I pray, Dear Lord, for the mind of Christ
And to show His love, which cannot be priced;
For the boldness of Paul I do desire,
With words and deeds, he did inspire.

To be humble like Israelite leader Moses,
Knowing all comes from You, unlike society proposes;
The faithfulness of Your servant Abraham
Would be a gift to cherish, like that of his ram.

Give me a heart after You, Oh, Lord,
Like on David the shepherd was nightly poured;
The wisdom of King Solomon, David's own son,
Should earnestly be sought by humans, each one.

Shadrach, Meshach, and Abednego in hot fire;
David with Goliath; Daniel's plight fearfully dire -
Faith and courage given them, no more than You've given me.
Your gifts given, please help me see.

I'm stuck with me, as long ago You planned,
This must be fine, since by Your mighty hand;
I can't be everything, like all from A to Z,
But I can be the me, You created me to be.

RUNNING FROM YOUR PLAN

I lay on my bed,
A heaped mass of human confusion;
I wanted to write,
But not at the expense of income and position.
Running from Your plan
For my life,
"My way, Lord! I want this,
Not that, for my life!"

"My Child, as you've heard,
There's no place to run, no place to hide;
The earth I created will not
Protect you from Me.
This temple of flesh I shaped
Cannot betray its Master Designer.
Your human will must
Be submitted to Me."

"Father, Father, I know not
How to not resist;
My life has been full
Of pain and struggle.
How else, but as a conqueror,
Can I respond?
Take my will and bend it,
As You will."

Judy A. Dees

The road to Nineveh is
One I've dreaded long.
Crowds of dissension and wantonness
Throng its glittered streets.
Battle worn and weary,
Fearful to face my task,
"Give me Your hand, Lord;
This battle belongs to You."

God Shows Love and Protection

SWEET HONEY

Tasting the sweet honey
Of Your grace and love
Cannot but draw me
To Your holy throne Above;
Never a love like this
Has lingered in my heart,
Never a grace like this
Could any man impart.

Only from You,
Loving Father in Heaven,
Could sweet melodies of
Unencumbered love be given;
Only from You,
Sacrificial Lamb and Savior,
Could a woman like me
Win love's favor.

Sweet honey given to
A world of pain and woe,
A healing balm to
The wayward and wicked foe;
Fountain of life,
Its soothing tendrils flow,
Sweet honey of God
Given His church to sow.

LIKE AN UNLOVED CHILD

Feeling so like an unloved child today,
Not hearing from my Father Above -
Not unlike one waiting in line long
For the colorful lollipop that never comes.

Despair overwhelming, wondering what I'd done wrong,
Emptiness lingering, long after wailing cry,
"Daddy, Daddy, where are You today?
I don't see Your face or feel Your presence near!"

"My Child, my Child, so soon have you forgotten!
I love you and could never ever leave you.
Why so anxious ridden have you become?
Did you take your eye off Me and put it on the storm?

We've been together for many miles now,
And though you've grown weary and discouraged,
I've never failed to restore and refresh
Your dust-covered, sun-scorched frailty.

Yes, a child - my child - you will ever be,
A sheep gently caressed in my dear Son's fold;
Known by Me since before you were born,
Hand chosen to someday reign with my Son up Above."

Verses From Above

JAD: Issues of childhood - rejection, neglect, abuse - definitely take a toll on one's relationship with and trust of God. A perfectly round mold of clay can become quite misshapen with a poke here, a squeeze there. Then, over time, that clay hardens in its misconstrued shape.

WHAT IS THAT TO ME?

Who am I to quarrel with nature's symphony swirl
Should She decide to dance a swing or do a jig?
What is that to me?

God rules from His throne Above, nature just His slave;
To do His bidding is Her one and only call.
What is that to me?

With Her mighty mountains and vast, deep seas,
Nature - a servant; I - a friend.
What is that to me?

JAD: Do we fail to realize just how awesome it is that Creator God considers us His friend?

CLAIM THOSE PROMISES!

Claim those promises, Christian Dear,
Illness and poverty no need to fear;
When walking down a path so drear,
Look up to Heaven; the way will be made clear.

Browbeaten and downcast, I lived for many a year,
Holy Bible by my side and prayer in my ear;
Now I read a different way, Holy Spirit near,
Rise up to victory! The world and Satan sneer.

Claim those promises! Our hearts they surely sear,
The truth they impart draws us ever near.
From His words and power never, never veer,
Don your sword and armor, and other battle gear.

GLORY OF THE LORD

Mine eyes did see the glory
Of the coming of the Lord
When, from rocky crags of this valley
Did I come;
Tender eyes that overflowed
With depth and compassion of love
Gave these pained, flickering lights
Hope of radiant new shine.

Stagnant tears of anguish
Replaced with fresh living water,
Etched, taunt, facial lines weathered
By stormy gales of life,
Relax in peaceful surrender
To Mighty Captain's command.

Freed now to roam in
My Lord's fair meadow garden,
Freed now to walk on
The depths of stormy seas;
Freed now to pass through
That Valley of Death - or its shadow -
Freed now to resist evil's fear:
My Lord is the great I AM!

Verses From Above

BIG!

Father God, my Lord and Master,
You hear my cries from lone, dark shadows;
You feel the pain my heart cannot escape,
You keep me from danger of falling.

Your big hand caresses my sobbing head,
Your big heart envelops my heart's broken pieces;
Your big feet carry me over desert heat and ocean storms,
Your big arms place me on solid rock of safety.

Your peace is the longing of my soul
When, day after day, some battle I face;
My weariness gets to the point of despair,
But still I must struggle from the enemy.

He is trying to get me, the Lord of Deep Darkness.
I once was his and influenced others his way.
Now, I have seen the Light from inside that pit;
To It I reach and show others its bright way.

Come rescue me, my Lord, from this foe of evil;
He would find me, but You can free me.
I know I am Yours, even when Death comes to visit me.
Were my porcelain walls exchanged for ones of clay and stone?

Judy A. Dees

JAD: Parts of some of these poems defy all grammatical sense or logic (For example, the last line of this poem); however, I do not dare alter the basic structure or content of the poems. Each word, each poem is designed for a specific person. I am just a hand.

FIRE GUIDE

As I stumble toward the Lake of Fire,
My eyes staid on You, my Guide,
I need not fear death - or scars;
With You in me, they pass me by.

Searing flames reduced to breaking waves,
Melting flesh exchanged for serene countenance;
Fear-laden eyes surrendered to assured twinkles,
Whimpering cries supplanted by smiles and laughter.

"When you pass through the blazing fires,
You need not be afraid of being burned;
When I call to you from the scorching inferno,
You need have no fear of being harmed."

Isaiah of the past followed the lead of his Master;
Are we not sheep of that same pasture?
The voice of another I am not called to hear.
Has He not promised to be my Good Shepherd and Guide?

Receive His Spirit's Fruit

FRUIT OF THE SPIRIT

In love, the charitable give,
With joy, the elated sing;

To peace, the tranquil cling,
In patience, the awaiting stand;

With kindness, the gentle serve,
To goodness, the benevolent aspire;

In faithfulness, the steadfast persevere,
With gentleness, the kind minister;

To self-control, the overcomers surrender,
For eternal life, the Christian lives.

Judy A. Dees

PEACE BE STILL

Peace be still. Peace be still.
How can one reach sweet level of peace
With the hustle and bustle of each busy day?
Peace is still; peace is quiet.

Peace is slowing long enough to take a seat,
Pausing a while to look at what's near;
It is casting cares and troubles to the wind
And letting go of breath you try to catch.

Peace longs to take a stroll by still waters
And listen to a bird's call or the lap of a wave;
It is basking in sunny warmth or cloudy cover;
Peace is waiting on God with no thought of utterance.

Doing nothing, having no place to go -
Have we forgotten what it is to be still?
Resting in solitude, interacting with not one soul,
Is finding peace with God and self a lost art?

THE RIVER

    Mighty, rushing River of God
   Floods my being with torrents of joy;
  Lulls peacefully along slumbering shores,
  Sweeps clean the silt from human souls.

  Leaves gurgling bubbles of love, peace, and joy
 Wherever its frills of current spread for deep rest;
  Wasteful sadness and destructive despair dissolve,
Disperses its chorus of hope, its melody of gladness.

    River revival of life and lover of my soul,
Take away the toil of my labor, the toll of earth's rust;
    Restorer of my soul, keeper of my gate,
     River of God, flow through me, then out!

Just Praise the Lord!

LIFTED TO YOU

I lift up my eyes to You,
Your way to follow when all I see is lies;
I lift up my ears to You,
Your gentle voice directs in life's bustling chaos.

I lift up my lips to You,
Your words come forth when feelings fail to trust;
I lift up my heart to You,
Your wisdom and workmanship cleanse and mend.

I lift up my hands to You,
You alone deserve my praise;
I lift up my voice to You,
You are the One I love and adore.

I lift up my head to You,
You are my Master and King;
I lift up my soul to You,
You are my life and one true love.

YOU AND ME, FATHER

Loving Father, above and around me,
Would that my words could express to You
All that You are and have been to me.
All the love I have, I give to You.

Each time I am in need,
You are there - and have been there -
Waiting for me to realize, in that need,
That only You can fill my every void.

Light of unseen path, River of flowing life,
Need in hungry souls, Rock of eternal salvation.
Father God! Lord Jesus! Holy Spirit!
Not even an inch from you let me stray.

JAD: Such hard times and struggles we may have to face - many valleys- especially when we respond to what we think God is telling us to do. But we are never alone.

I SAY I CANNOT SEE YOU

Father, I say I cannot see You;
Not a word of that is true.

I see You in the morning sky,
I see You in the light of night;
For sure, You're in a small child's smile
And knowing eyes of an aging friend.

Each petal of a flower,
Each leaf of a tree,
Caresses of the wind,
Warm touches of the sun.

How can I receive these gifts from You
And not know that my eyes, indeed,
Have beheld You in your glory?
If I say I cannot see you, not a word of that is true.

I LOOK BACK

Father, I look back at past days of my life,
Each day a new beginning, as I live life with You -
Daily work no longer a mere, mundane task,
Each bait of Satan left on its tempting line.

Father, I look back at past weeks of my life,
Each week growing stronger, as I walk your path of pain -
Desires seemingly fading, vision more pronounced,
My time for victory approaches, perpetual calendar turns.

Father, I look back at past years of my life,
A knowing smile turns my head to steady gait -
Mile, after rugged mile, turned into a beaten path
Walking by my Savior's side, hand-in-hand, Heaven bound.

JAD: Did life really exist before salvation? The days, weeks, and years pass differently; a person changes in ways never experienced before. One of my students asked, "Did you even have a life before you were saved?" After thought, I answered, "I thought so, but I'm realizing I really didn't."

WHATEVER

Whatever You want me
To think, Dear Lord,
My mind is Yours to do
As You please;
Each thought to bring captive
Before Your dear throne,
Renewed and rekindled
By Your holy, flaming sword.

Whatever You want me
To say, Dear Lord,
I give You my lips
To cleanse with hot coal;
My tongue, often sharper
Than a double-edged sword,
Is Yours for keeping
In your battle-worn sheath.

Whatever You want me
To do, Dear Lord,
My hands and feet
Are here to serve;
You made me and called me,
Then saved me by grace,
So whatever You desire,
My will is to please.

I LOVE YOU!

I love You, I love You, I love You!
My wonderful Lord and Savior Dear,
You are the height, depth,
And width of my being,
The living water without which
My soul would die.

I love You, I love You, I love You!
From a newborn babe in Christ You nurtured me,
From a life of sin and shame you rescued me;
From a hopeless eternity in deepest Hell
You saved me.
How can I not give you body and soul?

I love You, I love You, I love You!
The essence of my being lay I before You;
Take me, Lord, and make me wholly Yours.
For now that I am in You,
From You I cannot be apart.
I love You, I love You, I love You!

Verses From Above

JAD: Even as I type to get this first book to press, a second book of poetry is being found or written! I cannot fathom His great love! And if we, being evil, know how to give good gifts to our children, how much more can the Father in Heaven give to his children! Thank you, friend or brother/sister, for sharing these <u>VERSES FROM ABOVE!</u>

ON MAN AND NATURE

Ah, Lord God,
It is You who made the heavens and the earth
By Your great power
And by Your outstretched arm.
Nothing is too difficult for You!
(Jeremiah 31:17)

Verses From Above

FIFTY YEARS LATER

A sickly green frog
Once sat on a log,
Engaged in dialogue,
Enveloped in smog.
Said he to Ladybug,
"I need a big hug!
Right now, Bug,
Before my grave is dug."

How long they sat
There neither knew,
Enough breaths taken, though,
To get a sick flu;
"It must be another virus,"
Said Bug to Frog.
"The fifth for me,
In three months on this log."

Now a frog and bug should know
That pollution and its cloak
Will make for sick folk-
Maybe even make them croak;
Just move to a different tree,
Air clear so you can see,
Health and safety follow,
When no more toxin you swallow.

Judy A. Dees

JAD: I began this poem in sixth grade, almost fifty years ago. All I had down was, "There once was a frog that sat on a log…" Nothing else came - and it certainly did not after a classmate said, "Is that the best you can do?" Think back to something someone unthinkingly said to you that has affected you from then until now. I thought it was time to resolve this old poem. Its subject is an issue about which I have much passion: chemical pollution. I wonder what theme it might have had fifty years ago?

IN THE COMPANY OF UGLINESS

Crane, in whiteness and fragility,
A contrast to the mire,
Why would one such as you
Consort with such artifice of ugliness?
Is there beauty unknown
That escapes the visual eye?
Perhaps familiarity
That bonds with one inside?

Is there a depth
That hearts as one share
Or a comforting sense
That eludes aloof onlooker?
Crane, in whiteness and fragility,
A contrast to the mire,
Why would one such as you
Consort with such ugliness?

JAD: Parents often wonder why their beloved child chooses the company of undesirable peers. Like the beautiful white crane I observed, they (1) are attracted to the opposite (2) don't notice the differences (3) are more alike inside than outside (water seeks its own level; birds of a feather...) or (4) accept the differences.

TUMBLEWEED BLUES

Little tumbleweeds, blowing here and yon,
So tiny and seemingly unimportant,
But You made them, too.
Even people feel like little tumbleweeds,
So tiny and seemingly unimportant,
But You made them, too.

When I feel my tumbleweed blues,
I only need remember
The lesson I have learned:
If His eye is on
The sparrow and tumbleweed,
Then His eye is most certainly on me.

BARREN FIELDS OF THE HEART

Windswept, barren fields of the heart
Seeking solitude here, exposure there;
Divine plantation seeking kindred terrain,
Manifestation of one soul to another.

Amazed to stand : dust, wind, and sin - taking toll ,
Not unlike prairie swept hunchbacks;
Through forced gales of nature, economy, and politics
Victory dangled but assured to conquerors.

The foe cannot long force its tax,
Marvelous wonder to overcome!
I lift my head to fair breeze entangles,
Lofty, steep swishes past crowded fields.

Judy A. Dees

WEB OF DECEIT

Dawn's early morn weaves
A web of deceit;
Its burst of radiance reveals not
A trail of later darkness.
Its manner of innocence portrays
Little of hidden evil;
Lone, winding brook brings
Sweetness to morning's travail.

Sleeping inhabitants of
Nearby tranquil village
(Beckoned by slumber's sway)
Still repose,
As visitors of the night -
Their nasty lair forsaken -
Await entrapment of
Each silk threaded mesh.

JAD: The beauty of God's creation is daily marred by man's sinful nature. Ah! The innocence of nature - and children.

DELAYED DECAY

Winter's rancid flavor of mold and decay
Often echoes the spirit of a man of delay;
Every highway and byway paved
With many good intentions,
Progress and accomplishment
Marred with scared indentations.

Desiring to go everywhere but never going anyplace
Is this one who drags his feet
With every hindered pace;
Never doing more than dreaming in his mind,
Not knowing his gold possession,
Lying unmined.

Days full of disaster and confusion,
Weeks tiered with doubt and consternation;
Years wasted, passing him by,
Life spent.
This -
No money can buy.

Judy A. Dees

JAD: <u>Acres of Diamonds</u> (Russell Conwell) expounds upon the gifts of God to each person. One's unmined diamond is often in one's own backyard. To delay its search brings stagnation and decay. I didn't realize this poem was meant for me about the writing God had given me. What is your diamond mine or gold field that you have not discovered or mined?

FROM A BUTTERFLY TO A COCOON

When did it all begin,
This fear that remains such a part of me?
From whence did it come,
This fear that reigns over my life?

As a child, barefoot,
Roaming through the fields,
Stars in my eyes had not yet
Beheld this demon of fear.

Once a daring, young explorer,
Now, I dare not venture new territory.
I'd launch into orbit or play I had wings;
Now, my concrete soles won't leave their pad.

When did the transition occur?
Where was I
When I changed
From a butterfly to a cocoon?

JAD: A child's innocence and blind faith must surely entrust all to the Lord, for a child does not seem to even see, let alone comprehend, fears adults face.

FLOWER OF SOCIETY

She was a flower of society -
Nestled among rows of skyscraper tasks,
Watered underneath towering expectations,
Bedded in a wreath of rosebud perfection.

She was a flower of society -
Fertility encamped on a park river shore,
Futility veiled by shrouded city smog,
Superficiality diverted with gales of haughty laughter,
Humanity, in its travail, but a passing fancy.

She was a flower of society -
Wilted dreams limp from toxic ambivalence,
Faded laughter hollow from empty corridors,
Dried hopes brittle from hand fashioned idols.

She WAS a flower of society.

JAD: One of my devotionals prompted a reflection of days prior to my salvation. I had only recently read old journals of many years ago and was so amazed at how the Lord truly is faithful to complete the work He begins in us. Most of my life had been spent pleasing society rather than God. I WAS a flower of society!

PRAIRIE MAN OF OLD

Something longs to be said,
Lost in prairie vast,
"Speak now, or forever
Hold your peace!"
Are you speaking to those
Who will hear,
Or have you already spoken,
Then given up your will?

Are you remembering
Your soft, clad garment
Before highway and roadway
Left it scarred and torn?
Are you whimpering some
Sad lullaby, awaiting
The return of lost
Native American friends?

Are you longing to hear
The clamor of hooves and crunch of feet,
Rather than far and near
Rumble of rubber-clad iron?
Are you screaming to hear
The quietness of your thoughts
Amid humming and whirring wheels of progress noise?

Judy A. Dees

Could you not speak then - or now-
So forever held your peace?
But was it peace
You really thought you held?
Most of you is gone,
Prairie Man of Old;
As with mankind,
Does new always mean better?

SHARED WITH HIS CREATION

Raindrops -
Pelting against every object in the way,
Cast a shadow of resistance
To nature's own way;
Cleaning residue from Heaven
Shared by God with His creation,
Mellowing earth's dryness,
Refreshing man's arid heart.

Rainbow fair -
Stretching to connect earth and sky,
Almost as if it played a hand
In drenching rain;
Stretching to relieve itself
Of bounteous duty,
Fanning radiant color to say
All work for the day is done.

Wind -
Swirling in and around to do its finish work,
Sweeping dry trees and land
After rain's visit;
Blanketing man and beast
In soothing cradle,
Paving the way for sunlight
To bring its glorious array.

TUMBLEWEED LIFE

Tumbleweed, tumbleweed! Tossed oft by prairie winds,
You gather speed but gain no ground;
Blown here and yon 'til almost gone:
Such is the life of the faithless.

Battered and broken by roadway express,
Left in median or ditches' clutches;
Adorning automobile grilles or truck bumpers:
Such is the life of the wayward.

Woe is the poor weed whose tumble meets with fence,
Caught in its piney tips or webbed veins;
Snared and held captive till winds of change abound:
Such is the life of the victim.

Great Maker of tumbleweed plant and people,
Watchful eye and helpful hand so near,
Can set them free or mend their broken spines:
Such is the life of the redeemed!

AFTERNOON MOUNTAIN SHOWER

Rain blanket of gentle mist kisses my face;
Rising to meet its cooling touch, beauty surrounds me.
Nothing compares to afternoon mountain shower.

Glistening splendor bursts forth in panoramic freshness,
One shower follows another; downpours bring occasional rest.
Summer's mountain day is at glorious end!

Judy A. Dees

MR. MOON

Pardon me, Mr. Moon in night sky,
How can you be there so high?

Looking down on earth below
Night light smiles bright but slow.

Changing busy pace to restful calm,
Like lyrics and music of a Bible psalm.

SNOW BEAUTY

Snow Beauty,
Swirling your way round man and beast
Leaving white blanket splendor
Wherever your feet rest;
Pillowed softness for
Lone, travel- worn critters,
Shrouded enchantment vision
Greeting watcher's delighted eye.

Bringing smiles on faces
Of outdoor playsters,
Leaving glows on cheeks
Of excited children;
Prompting cheers from mouths
Of playful youth,
Assuring peace in hearts
Of mellowed elders.

Snow Beauty,
Envelop me in your cloak of pure white!
I welcome your frost tap
On my waiting face.
Your magical gusts fill me
With warm tender glow;
Come rest your wintry delight
At my cabin's front door.

SNOW

Pillowed snow cloud
Hovers above my head,
Just waiting for His command,
"Let the snow begin!"

Each crystal flake,
Awaiting its destined place,
Will surely fall, then call
Me out to play.

A snowman we'll make
To greet each passerby;
A sleigh ride we'll take
On long and frosty morn.

Snowmobiling valleys and hills
Will be such wonderful fun;
Snow ice cream tops it off -
This joyful, glorious day.

DREAMER'S FEAST

Lighted path through nature's snowy swirl,
Domicile parade dances to dark midnight whirl;
Destination embraced with tinseled icy procession,
Dreamer's feast of imagination,
A most natural obsession.

LITTLE SNOWFLAKE

Little snowflake
Playing with other snowflake friends,
Swirling in circles,
Making pretty designs on the ground;
Squealing on rollercoaster rides to my back yard,
Little snowflake
Blanketing white beauty as far as I can see.

Little Snowflake,
Have you a daddy and mommy
To protect from wintry wind - blast's harm?
Have you a sister or brother
For play all the day long?
Little Snowflake,
Have you a welcome home when day is done?

SON - GLOW RADIANCE

Snuggled in warm bed of radiant Son glow,
Knowing He who made me is faithful and true
To do just as He promised, His Holy Word due,
Protecting fragile flower from sundry, pestilent foe.

Knowing He who created all is on His mighty throne
Looking down from Above, away from sin lurks;
Her Master to please, as she dutifully works
Each blessed day to overcome temptations lone.

In preparation for fall's autumn silence hibernation,
Bedded down for life's cyclic, wintry freeze;
Awaiting spring's awakening lure of balmy breeze,
Bud and blossom, in radiant splendor, face summer Son's liberation.

BIRD OF FAITH

If His eye is on the sparrow,
How much more it rests on me!
Little bird covered with mere feathers,
I - made in the image of my Father.

Knowing not its food for the day,
Worried not, for it will be fed;
Perched high, in one of plenteous trees,
From its enemies - safe - through long night.

Tizzed and fretted, I oft toss and turn,
Anxious about toilsome days to come;
Had I the faith of one little bird,
Head on pillow, day would peacefully fade.

JAD: One night I was - again - tossing and turning, worried about tomorrow's demands. My pillow just couldn't be fluffed enough, so I hit it. At that moment, I heard a bird chirp (at night?!) That it had more faith than I seemed to be its soft reminder.

I AM THE WORM

Oh, that the early rooster did crow innocently,
Knowing not it was Your will he spat;
And the braying donkey spoke to man.
So surely, for this worm You will find a use.

No attributes can I boast on my own;
Like the worm, I only help till the soil.
I slither and inch my way on the ground,
Then bury my head at the least little fright.

Crush me easily with mouth, hand, or foot;
My gushing and crying heard far in the air.
Part of me lies flat, wounded by man,
But eyes look upward to my Savior and Friend.

God, history records Your use of weak and small;
Weakness looms over me larger than my minuteness.
But greater are You who is in me,
So worm, donkey, rooster - or me - it matters not at all.

Judy A. Dees

KNOW

Mountain top high, creeping over horizon's face,
Greets weary travelers with awesome hope:
Know that in life's bleak barrenness
Lies soaring beauty and strength from Above.

Time can seem unbearable, troubles that never end,
But know that, if down the road you keep plodding,
Rest will come; restful end will arrive.
Lift up your eyes to Maker of Heaven and Earth!

Verses From Above

PRAIRIE HUMMMMM

As destiny would have it,
Many years unfold.
From my vantage point
It's been foretold,
Lives of men and women
Passing prairie fields.
Plod and pull, wish
And wail, ponder and pray.

Song and dance but a dream
In the mind's sky,
Trying to survive,
Not pausing to wonder why.
Children of the Plain,
Men and women of the times.
Blood and brevity, hope
And happenstance, beauty and brawn.

Miracle of miracles,
The fact that they stood.
A fact they accepted,
Just knew that they could.
From labor to rest,
From vision to faith.
Courageous and civil, gregarious
And grateful, content and complete.

Judy A. Dees

JAD: I do not understand the syntax of this one, but it came, so I wrote. It speaks to my spirit and soul but not to my mind!

CONFETTI ENCHANTMENT

Flowered array of yellow, blue, and white
Dance and sing in prairie choir.
Swirls of confetti enchantment dot meadow plains;
Romantic madness lures watchful eye.

Ah! The splendor of deference, wisp of beauty hidden.
Lone deer trail in floral blanket cover,
Visual comfort for tired, anxious eye,
Whisked away by prairie fire or winter's chill.

Verses From Above

SUNFLOWER GIRL

Your season is ore, dear Sunflower Girl,
Head hanging down after use and abuse;
At one time, so lovely - head held high -
Colors bright and cheery for all who'd pass by.

Is this a prank of nature: that all are but for use?
Then why be created, if only but to fall?
Spring and summer bring warm, soft breeze,
Fall, then winter, follow with cold, hard freeze.

It may seem that life has no purpose,
But that cannot be true;
The moment you were planted, Someone had a plan:
Your use, not abuse, for the end good of man.

JAD: What evil means for bad, God means for good.
ALL things can work together for good.

REAP OF INNOCENCE

Sunflower fields beckon passersby,
Camera in hand through unfamiliar grasses,
For a privileged glimpse of woebegone beauty -
An unplanned encounter with freedom swaying.

Innocent maidens boast their innate rhythm,
Flaunt their unaffected beauty,
Graciously adorn the otherwise bleak terrain -
Bright, smiling faces lifted up to their Maker.

Unaware, as so often the naïve,
That threshing time was near;
For another's use was their life given -
An aftermath of chaff and stubble.

Like any other weed in a barren, unhealthy field.

Verses From Above

JAD: Like the sunflower, the beauty of innocence can be seen in every child, so naïve and trusting - until he or she becomes an object of someone's use.

Why several poems about the prairie? On our vacations to Colorado, I found it very difficult to get through Kansas. I thought it was flat and dull. I asked God to show me the beauty of Kansas. He did! Not only did He show me Kansas through His eyes, as one of His created beauties, but also He showed me its historical significance and economic importance to our country. Then He showed me how His creations man and nature were alike in so many ways.

Judy A. Dees

SILENT LASS

Prairie flowers sprinkled thus far,
Who are you trying to reach?
What are you trying to say,
Clad in your domesticated beauty?

A tale of sorrow, pain, and woe
Or delightful cadence from fragrant mouth flow;
Tidbits of gossip long refrained,
Spoken long last, after years detained.

Silent lass from prairie wildfire escapes
To safe serenity of pasture bliss;
Breath of freshness in morning's mist,
Restful evening, one sunset away.

JAD: Sometimes one who is silent is left alone, almost invisible to a rampaging destroyer.

FADED DREAMS

Moonswept sky of star-studded night,
What is it you are trying to tell me?
How oft, in long ago moments, did we exchange
Secrets and dreams from hearts full of hope?

Do you try to send me your faded dreams
On the blazing trail of a shooting star?
Or have you hidden them, somehow,
Amid Milky Way's galactic maze?

And what of me? With whom do I consort?
The sway of bustle shrouded in crowded places,
Perhaps those tedious chores that never end.
What has really taken me from you?

The truth could be no clearer than moonlit sky spray:
I am the culprit, my freedom willingly given.
No fight for you did I chance to take,
Now, a price I pay unrelentlessly.

JAD: Dreams ARE important - and a part of who one is. When a person becomes so busy that dreams are lost (or, at least, fade), something in that person's life is missing. Something Joyce Meyer wrote (whether or not her own words, I do not know) was, "I'd rather have a dream that failed than to never have had a dream at all." Dreams are what I've held to since youth; some haven't materialized- yet - but many have. This book is one of my biggest and oldest dreams, one I've had since eighth grade or before, my classmate Bill House reminded me. "As a man thinks, so is he." (Proverbs 23:7) Understand?

POETIC COLLAGE

Like poets gathered upstream
In river bend sway,
Is a schoolhouse of children
On snowy, wintry day;
Breathless with excited thoughts
Of testy anticipation,
Waiting, waiting,
For an invitation to begin play.

A voice heralding
Nature's release to mankind
Echoes sentiments
To those near and far;
Just a bit longer will it
Ask you to tarry -
Not any longer than is needed
To finish its course.

Rhythmic tune
Celebrates nature's fancy;
Melodious wail beckons
The listening ear to come forth;
Sweet-stir silence pauses
Wherever it pleases,
Serene assurance secures
Surveillance of the artist's poetic collage.

PRAIRIE GROVE

Prairie Grove,
Do you not feel all alone?
You are stuck in the middle of nowhere
Against cloudless sky,
Your only company a herd
Of cattle in need of shade
Or a flock of birds seeking
Perch for weary wings.

Prairie Grove,
How do you survive the wind?
Bleak, barren fields of harvest
Leave you to face that force;
Stinging dust snips
Every branch and limb,
Twisting winds stretch and bend
Until you lose your shape.

Prairie Grove,
What is it you have to tell?
Maybe that historic, steepled church
Nestled safe near your side
Once carried a tale of sweet endearment
You could recall;
Surely warriors, soldiers, or farmers
Who have used you as respite
Made such impression on you
That could be interestingly shared.

Verses From Above

Prairie Grove,
What is that you see?
Do you see a fading nation,
Once a splendid light,
Forcing its way toward
Destruction and deprivation,
Mile after momentous mile
Of repetitious insanity?

Prairie Grove,
Someday you will enter a time of rest
From man-made pollutants,
By-products of modern progress;
From malnutrition and poison,
Those instant fertilizer foods;
From greed and deceit,
Hallmarks of business and industry.

PRAIRIE MAIDEN

Lovely sunflower maidens
Of prairie ever sublime,
I missed your visitation,
Never dreaming harvest was near;
Your field-enveloped artistry
Lasts not long enough.
Radiant faces as yours,
A welcome sight to travelers shorn.

Was your awakening
A blessed sight to behold -
Vast playground beholding
Making you desirous to sprout and grow,
Countless hours of sunlight
From prairie magnified sun,
And wind spurts most plenteous
For your summertime ballet of fun?

Was your life one of
Radiant hues and pleasantry days?
I hope it was not one of
Stormy skies and blighty ills;
Perhaps it was like mine -
A sure-fire mix of good and bad -
And the balance of both left you
Standing straight, tall, and strong.

Verses From Above

Ah, the time of harvest
Came all too soon, I see.
Even though I missed you,
That you were here can be seen;
You existed in abundant individualism
For all the world to see.
Although another will grow in your place,
None can be the same as you.

THRESHING TIME

For many years I beheld your splendor -
Breezeful sway in my garden of beauty -
Laughter flowing, frolicking freely
Midst my sisters of the field.
Then came threshing time.

Head bent low from its former lifted state,
Eyes downcast not wishing to see my fate;
Leaves of green turned to misty brown,
Petals falling one-by-one.
Life in each was spent.

Reluctantly, I relinquish my steadfast staid;
My time to die is near, the life I had, fading;
Grim Reaper beckons,
Ever ready to do his bidding.
I harken to the call of the thresher.

Unlike sister sunflower, life spent in a single year,
Joy and happiness abounded - a decade more or less.
Few experience this mountaintop high,
As, hand-in-hand, we strolled.
My Savior and I exulted.

In Heaven, I'll meet my Love, never to part again;
Illness, despair, and death
Never a victor there.
For this trodden flower girl,
A final resting place.

VIBRANT DEMISE

Daffodil lily sat in truffled splendor,
Directing her musical ensemble
Midst swaying, vibrant leaflets;
Choral voices echo
Spring and summer arrival.
Gentle breeze and soaking showers
Send cheer to thirsty maiden.

Gracing dainty corners of
Chic restaurant congregation,
Greeting early risers in solitary homely abode,
Announcing congratulations to
Chagrined excellence proclaimed,
Smiling love's simple splendor
To one's favored personage.

Elegance, fragrance, beauty, affection, celebration -
Personified in nature's field
Of floral visage;
Oh, to exemplify the full extent
Of usefulness and integrity,
Then accept the reality
Of vibrant life's grass demise.

GARDEN OF ABUSE

I will repay you
For the years
The locusts have eaten.
(Joel 2:25a)

Garden of Abuse. How could anything as hideous
as abuse ever be referred to as a garden? A garden
does not usually begin on its own; it must be planted.
Such is the Garden of Abuse. Its bad beginning is
from the hand and acts of sinful man; its ending is
from the hand and acts of righteous God. What Satan
and evil man meant for bad, God meant for good. God
can make the uneven, even, and the crooked, straight.
He WILL (if we let Him) restore to us what the locusts
of destruction took from us, as a child or as an adult.

Through my own and others' life experiences and
through personifying the course of nature, I've seen
a most unique and wondrous garden emerge from fields
of stubble, heaps of hardened dirt, and piles of crusted
rocks. Their beautiful heads have wound their ways
through the tangled weeds and prickly thorns, as they
courageously broke through the crusted ground cover that
held them captive season after season. The crop? A
hearty, splendorous garden amid a field of abuse.

These poems explore issues surrounding abuse and the
hearts of its victims, or they offer a type of hope for the
survivors. Many of the flowers and beauties in this garden
have human names; they could be anyones - mine, yours, or
others we know.

GARDEN OF ABUSE

Children come to my place
Physically battered and abused;
When truth is made known,
They, often, are the ones accused.
Some play the parental role,
Others, lost children of neglect;
Their parents children themselves
Unable to maturely reflect.

Here sits one prim and proper child,
From a prim and proper house.
Who would believe the verbal onslaught
That left him quiet as a little mouse?
His twin victim sibling
Had taken quite a different turn:
Acid daily cursings
Released his rage in a steady burn.

Stranger, still, are
Ones sexually used;
These you try to label,
But they are all confused.
Some act out or rebel against
This use and abuse;
Others refrain -
And become the elusive muse.

Verses From Above

Garden of abuse -
How will it grow?
To prune it or weed it
Brings out old, hidden woe;
But to nurse it and heal it
Seems a most unfamiliar task.
Let God's love and your care
Remove this ugly, unwanted mask.

BETRAYAL

Penciled paper betrays my inner self,
That childhood figure evading
Crude elements of humanity;
Sister to the wind, privy to its beckoning call,
A lass so fragile the flowers befriend her.

What brutality dared torment her thus
That she one day lost her sister and friends?
Paled in comparison,
When previous contrast would suffice,
Lonely waif walked where fair maiden did dance.

A glimpse of her my tired eyes have beheld.
Why, at this age, should she seek to return?
Ah! Age is but a
Physical restriction of life;
Youth, God's gift to the spirit of man.

I rid myself of this elongated betrayer!
Each time I embrace it, She gusts forth -
Whether in gales of laughter
Or breezes of tranquility -
Ink well of the past smearing my scroll of today.

JAD: One might think she has hidden or lost that inner child of the past, only to find her (or his) unexpected visitation via a work of art: drama, writing, art, or another form of self expression.

FETAL PAYMENT PLAN

Who do you think you are,
Taking my life so people won't know?
You played the game and lost,
But it is I who must pay your debt.
You think you're untouched
In your make-believe world;
Little do you know, my Dear,
About this insidious payment plan.

The hole inside you
That used to be me
Gets larger and emptier,
As time passes by;
Though my body was
Torn, ripped, and destroyed,
My spirit still lives;
That can't be denied!

That child playing
In the nearby park -
Does she look like me,
Like what you thought I'd be?
Or do I look like the child
You unceasingly see when,
Through long, unending nights,
You gaze into the mirror of your soul?

Year following tormented year,
You push my memory aside.
Life becomes a blur;
Everywhere are constant reminders of me.
Where is this person
You once knew and understood?
Did only an unimportant part of you die
When, from me, you were set free?

Then comes the day
When your deed you realize.
You can run no more;
Nothing can you hide.
Abysmal agony gnaws
At the door of your soul -
This aborted fetus,
With its infinite payment plan.

JAD: For every woman who has aborted a child (or plans to): This was one of the most important decisions you will ever make in your life. It was one that will affect you, directly or indirectly, the rest of your life. Abortion affects the body, soul, spirit, emotions, and mind of a woman; it affects her ability to be a wife and mother. Abortion is not normally categorized as abuse, but, in my opinion, it is major abuse - first, to the unborn child and next, to the woman herself. She may be more educated about abortion than in past years, but she still does not see the whole picture until years and years later. Know that God can restore the locusts of abortion, too.

Judy A. Dees

PROSTITUTED INNOCENCE

Little child frolicking free
Unaware, unaware of this beast you must flee;
Helpless and hurt, tormented and tried,
The one you loved most
Was that beast when unleashed.

Your tilting laughter and smiling eyes
Would soon lose all gaiety - seemingly, even life;
The frail body so innocently made
Had become an object
Of depravity and abuse.

Tucked infinitely in the recesses of her mind,
Tumultuous life of shame and guilt, tossed in the wind;
For not at all did she know that her promiscuity
Was merely a replay
Of her prostituted innocence.

JAD: Why so much sexual immorality in today's society? Is it that mankind is so wicked - or might it possibly be that the promiscuous teen or adult is merely acting out a young history of sexual abuse?

SPOONFED IMAGINATION

Spoonfed imagination,
Daring not one bite of reality -
Its insipid taste unpleasing
To one in such delicate state,
Its stark panorama unbearable
To one in sheltered bliss;
Spoonfed imagination: alive,
But never living beyond shallow moor.

Spoonfed imagination,
Where did you learn to pick and choose?
Did you hide under
Tables laden with fear,
Eating only the crumbs
Of another's careless mess,
Or on the bed of woe, eating
What was dished you by predator's appetite?

Perhaps a lifelong
Road of violence
Taught you well
Its hide-and-seek;
Spoonfed imagination,
Dare you change your eating utensil?
The slice of life you're missing
Might well be freedom's recipe.

Judy A. Dees

JAD: Children who are abused or neglected often find an escape from their reality in the world of imagination. True freedom comes, however, upon facing that fearful reality." The truth will set you free."(John 8:32)

I NEVER KNEW

I never knew that I was someone special:
No other person on earth
With my weaknesses and strengths,
No living being
With the same likes and dislikes -
A unique and individual being,
Fashioned by God in His love.

I never knew that I was someone innocent:
My sweet soul waiting
For life's buds to bloom,
Trustful of both sheep and wolves,
Knowing not which to avoid -
Created in my mother's womb,
Impressionable as the snow white dove.

I never knew that I was someone lovely:
A fun-loving little girl
With sparkles in her eyes,
A laugh unlike any other
Specially created for me -
Fearfully and wonderfully made
By Father looking down from Above.

Judy A. Dees

JAD: Few people accept and love themselves as they are. Because they have no idea of their true identity, many hide behind different masks; others make decisions that harm or destroy themselves. If we could see ourselves as God sees us, true self acceptance would be the result.

Verses From Above

BLESSED EXCHANGE

So you know not the truth from a lie
When, as a child, perceptions had to die.

You're drawn to ones who treat you like tatter,
Knowing not, as a youth, that really you did matter.

En route to my past, I noticed a change:
It did not last! What a blessed exchange!

A sense of familiar feelings lingered, underlying
Some vibrant spring from which poured life, so satisfying.

Reverberations of a melancholic tune
Gave rhythmic lyrics to which I'd become immune.

With sad dissonance, yet in one accord,
My mind and fancy part company as I sit to record.

JAD: We do NOT have to stay in the pain or negative conditions of our past. With the Lord, we become a new creation!

WALLS

What secret lies within me, Lord,
That keeps my all from You?
What keeps me from accepting fully
The truth of Your love for me?
Why do I find it hard to trust
The One who can save my soul?
Why do I still feel forgotten,
As if I'm all alone?

Is it sin in me from which
I'm still not set free?
A willful sin of disobedience,
One from which I will not flee?
Or one of which I'm unaware
And just can't seem to see?
Perhaps in rebellion and divination
Laden feet are stuck to me?

Could it be, Lord,
A sin from past years or days?
A resentment held fast,
Fearful of repentant release?
Or a wrong deed done another
And pride prevents repair?
Perhaps a long abiding lie
Bound heart deep, its presence unaware?

Verses From Above

If not all this, Lord,
That keeps my wall intact,
Is it the child of my youth,
Clay mold torn from abuse and neglect?
This does much toward tarnishing
Even the most unique and stoic pattern of clay.
I know not, Lord, the cause of thick walls,
But You, in Your might, know the answers to all.

FROM ONE WHO HURTS

Dismal days of celebrated fancy,
Your call of misery beckons,
Its wiry nodules protruding;
Some poor, miserated being -
Only longing to be touched.
Unknowingly, she causes to vanish
That which she most desires.

Elusive friendships wander farther yet,
Creeping around each shadow
Of pain - waiting -
Having learned that
Getting too close to vermin
Will the mind wither
In vanishing smoke.

Oh, you who are full
Of misery and woe!
Reach out and touch -
Without your searing torch;
Sit down and commune -
Without your insipid tongue;
Cast out those shadowed demons,
Then watch the pain retreat.

JAD: So true is a saying, "When a person deserves love the least is when he needs it the most." Hurting people hurt others! The rejection that follows is the very thing he or she least desires.

CHILD OF ABUSE

Precepts and consequences -
Budding in life's evil travail;
Doomsday and sorrow -
Awaiting the lost child of abuse.

Twisted and tormented -
The altered minds of children used;
Fragmented and wasted -
A life so precious, sacrificed.

Bloodshed and tears -
Inhabiting some poor, lost soul;
Grief and hopelessness -
Season of finality, a riptide storm.

Repaired and restored -
Redeeming Savior of children broken;
Peaceful and content -
Facing the rest of life renewed.

REJECTION

Firmly rooted deep inside me,
Rejection entwines; it won't let go.
As a child, I embraced it with naivete,
Oblivious to its poisonous tentacles.

It wound with deceit its way to my knees,
And youthful innocence allowed it a grip;
Noticing a limp, I looked all around,
But so used to these cords, I continued my way.

Teenage years brought several falls;
By then, solid chains wouldn't let me part.
Feelings became hidden, for fear of many tears;
Now firmly seeded was a bed of insecurity.

Life progressed; my heart became entangled.
Weary and tired, from heavy ball and chain carried,
My walk got longer and harder, extra burdens I bore.
When did it begin? Where does it end?

Did I hear of Savior Jesus, who can a captive free?
Will His truth give freedom to such a one so bound?
In Light for me to see, He exposed this rooted chain.
Now He leads me by still waters; secure in Him I am.

SPIRIT OF FEAR

Spirit of Fear, lodged inside me deep,
Release your hold; fresh air I need to breathe.

Fear of man and what he will think,
Fear of failure and the shame it may bring;
Fear of success, public recognition of my name,
Fear of rejection and its pain-filled spear.

Fear of loss in this empty, hollow life,
Fear of gain with its unfamiliar change;
Fear of love, the prospect of risk it brings,
Fear of hate, its shunning recoil to embrace.

Lord, help me see through this din of fear,
The real me who has no reason to fear.

TANGLED

Surely I once felt so loved and accepted
To now feel so deeply insecure and rejected;
Or have I always felt unworthy, unwanted,
And it merely grew, as I grew, leaving me taunted?

It gathered moss as I rolled it along;
Taking it with me, I could never belong.
My mole hill became a mountain thicket,
Making me lose my way; I could not lick it!

One day, a friend came by my side.
"You CAN get out! The devil has lied!"
We toiled and cut 'til brush was all clear;
I was on a mountain top with One so, so dear!

INNOCENT GLEE

Parading the crowd
With youthful, innocent glee,
One glimpse of her hero
Would cost her to eternity;
Dancing around the circle of men,
She went merrily;
Kerosene lantern silhouetted
Her little body bent.

One aroused, then another
In the crowd of drunken men.
Then something happened
That made her cry out loud;
Goodbye to her dance, farewell to her song
Her innocent glee lay on damp ground.
Tattered and torn, crept she back to camp.
"Honey, what's wrong?" asked Mom with concern.

Huddled in far small corner
Of the truck bed where they slept,
A blank and empty expression left,
As she lay down and wept.
Memories of that unforgettable night
Left her little sweet mind,
Until decades later, they emerged for late night visits.

Judy A. Dees

Why do I keep replaying
The memory of that scene?
I see a lighted lantern
And a circle of friendly men.
Why can I see no farther
But skip right to the end?
Was it that time in between
When I lost my innocent glee?

DADDY, DADDY

Daddy, daddy! Why do you hurt me so?

Am I so bad that stripes must be left on my back?
Am I so stupid that answers are yelled to my questions?
Am I so worthless that I'm worked hard as a slave?
Am I so ugly that I have no pretty clothes?
Am I so unpleasant that my company is seldom desired?
Am I so unimportant that I'm treated as a possession?
Am I so lazy that I work only 12 hours each day?

Do you hate me? Why was I even born?

I was told that I was a miracle baby.
I was told that I was wanted so badly.
I was told you took me everywhere with you.
I was told you were so proud of me.
I was told I was Daddy's Little Princess.

Was I told lies? Why such a change?

From a princess to a pauper -
From a flower to a weed -
From a somebody to a nobody -
From a life to a death.

O, LITTLE CHILD

O, Little Child,
Were you two or three,
When robbed of youthful
Innocence and glee?

You are not easily remembered.
Is this because of pain,
Or might something be missing
From my muddled brain?

I had always thought
You must be undesirable or mean;
Else why were you rejected
And left, too often, unclean?

Your big brown eyes
Were those of a sad puppy.
Was it hard to smile
When your throat felt swollen and lumpy?

The long, stringy hair
That fell in your face -
Did that help cover
Your feelings of disgrace?

Hour after hour of sitting alone
In the back of a store -
Could you help but feel anything
Except rotten to the core?

Verses From Above

Times of playing make-believe
And wishing you weren't you -
How could you know then
That wishes DO come true?

Quite the dreamer, ever a deceiver,
Your wish now in play -
Did you know to think then
That your emotions would decay?

You became stunted
And locked up in a maze -
Part mummy, part zombie,
Long over ten thousand days.

JAD: Child abuse is too common; actually, it is rampant. All abuse - emotional, verbal, physical, sexual - takes its toll. When does it begin? Very early - from infancy on. The most devastating, sex abuse, is most usually begun between ages three and eight. Abusers are usually people close to the children. Insane!

Judy A. Dees

PAST CORRIDOR HALLS

Matriarch of past corridor halls
Marches forward, with heavy laden heart;
Timeless effort spent, not even pocket change to spare.
Where are the children? Who took them away?

"Kids will be kids," a famous saying quotes.
But where are the children, passing years gone by?
Torn and wasted by seagulls of some ocean swamp,
Is not one remnant left to gather?

"How can they be reached?" she ponders -
Those innocent victims of days gone by;
How can they be found in such a thicket,
Fenced by pain and anger, distrust and fear?

Yes, this garden of abuse can be used
To bring the lost and dying to our Master Healer;
His hands and feet were torn and scared,
His heart and soul have also rent in pain.

He came to seek and save the lost;
To the hurt and weary comes this Prince of Peace;
She turns and leaves her medley of memories,
Knowing where there was no hope, there is now ALL hope!

Verses From Above

JAD: I taught school for almost 25 years. Always, there were students, many crying for my help or love. Now, in my life, there are none. This poem must be an extension of the dreams of my beloved profession.

DARKNESS POUNDING

Darkness pounding at my door,
What, for me, does it have in store?
Madness, melancholy, depressive lies,
For me, it stalked; redemption cries.

Are you the culprit of sleepless nights?
Have you no respect for human rights?
Do you think yourself a god on kingly throne?
Slink back into your shadows; this is God's light zone.

REMINISCING

Reminiscing. A release for torrents of past years' rain,
A celestial verbage of
Muddled fears, tears, and regrets;
Faded cloth of youth's tapestry on wheels,
Moon dance of war waged
Against haunts of discolored shadows.

Vague memory of enchanted childhood dreams,
Painful smile for
Disillusioned innocence at play;
Ever reaching toward unidentified star of night,
Settling softly in snuggled shelter
Of make-believe lies.

Eruption of truth, surfacing to expose new foundation:
Freedom - from survival, fancies, and schemes -
To face lies
That were there all along,
To see reality shedding light on a path
You never knew existed.

JAD: Looking back on one's life (often during parenthood) can sometimes bring to light unrealized or unknown truths that have been lying in wait to be unearthed.

LIFTED

You lifted me from that mire
In which I had been stuck,
Saved and Heavenbound I am,
For sure not mere luck;
You had called my name
From the time I was three,
But sin and shame caused me
To constantly flee.

Inflicted childhood,
Harvested troubles of youth,
Finalized slowly into great loss
Of the truth;
My eyes blinded
Until I was reborn,
A heart inside,
Battered and torn.

Lamer and lamer 'til not a step
Would I take,
"I need a Savior!
My chains, only He can break!"
Deeper and deeper into that stench
Did I sink,
Until one day, what I beheld
Made me unable to think.

Who was this peering at me
From mirrored pane?
Only the silhouette of a little one
In much, too much, pain.
Eyes - lost and empty,
Vision - gazed and unseeing;
Face - masked with gauntly parlor,
Smile - faded paste peeling.

That was then;
This is now.
Glimpses of her sadness
Bring a melancholic vow;
Not one wish of my heart
Desires that yesteryear.
I lift my eyes and march,
No earthly reason to fear.

JAD: It matters not into which pool of mire we've fallen. The Lord can lift us out! (Psalm 40)

SON-FILLED RADIANCE

Dazed inferno of listless mind -
Trying to forget searing pain,
Trying to lessen stinging words,
Trying to hide vulnerable tears.

I want to face that pain,
I want to feel that emotion;
I want to find that path to acceptance,
I want to experience peace beyond understanding.

Too many years lost to faded memory,
Too many moments bound up in dazed ice;
Fear of fear, fear of heartache,
Leaving their void in fragmented mind.

To be alive is to see past blinding tears,
To walk steadfastly through valleys blind;
To reach upward from smoke - screened walls,
To step forward in Son-filled radiance beaming.

WHAT THE LOCUSTS HAD TAKEN

Heaped in a muddle
Of tears and torn innocence,
Wondering what
She had done to cause this;
Where are You, God?

Forever losing that
Most delightful laugh and twinkling eye,
Why is she crying on the inside
But dry-eyed on the outside?
Where are You, God?

Dancing feet now lead-laden stones,
Spontaneous play stifled with fear;
Where is she hiding?
Where did she go?
Where ARE You, God?

Rumbling through her youthful years,
Stumbling down the path to adulthood,
Stagnating in the pool of existence;
She never knew that God
WAS there, all along.

Judy A. Dees

He was the One
Who pulled her from death,
The One who kept
Her eyes from blindness,
The One who assured her survival -

And the One who was now ready to restore to her
What the locusts had taken from her in her youth.

A MOTHER'S HAND

Don't tell me
I have nothing to lose,
For things as they are
Can only confuse;
Embittered heart
Of one so young,
Only wanting love,
To his mother clung.

"I'm too busy working
For society's eyes;
Sorry I can't help you
With your childish cries.
I love you, Child,
But I love me more;
If you'd realize that,
Yourself you would less abhor."

A mother's hand still rocks
The cradle of humanity;
Some, no longer strong and loving,
Rock evil, hatred, and insanity.
Where is the mother
Who cares for the child?
She's under the bill stack,
Asleep where they're piled.

Judy A. Dees

JAD: Perhaps the most common abuse today is that of negligence, a type of emotional abuse. "Nothing begats nothing," is an old saying. So true! How can we expect people to give away (love, kindness, concern) that which they don't have to give - because they never received it.

WHERE DO I BEGIN ?

To know to do good
And not do it is sin;
I look around and think,
"Where do I begin?"

More pain than ever
In this old world,
Oh, my weak, weary shoulders
Become stiff and curled.

Anger unresolved
Soon billows as rage;
On babes, dear children,
And each other - a savage wage.

Violence rampant -
One hardly feels safe;
A danger to all society,
Not just the homeless waif.

Crime no more
Confined to the streets,
Lives of innocent victims
It often depletes.

Ravages of abuse
Eventually become revealed;
Perpetuation of each incident
Upon society is spilled.

Judy A. Dees

"Where do I begin?
I must ask again;
It all begins and ends
In different types of sin.

There's only one answer
To the state we are in;
On our knees before Jesus,
A work He will begin.

ONCE ENSLAVED

Once enslaved by demons many-fold,
Chains entwined 'round spirit and soul;
Knowing nothing different than misery and woe,
Daily seeking reprieve,
Not knowing where to go.

Seemingly destined to a life of despair,
Blinded and fettered by the Prince of Dark;
Life withering away,
Hope slithering through cracked façade,
Myself - a vanishing mirage, a decomposing silhouette.

Drawing nearer my fated destiny
On my final walk down the freeway of demise,
Something passing caught
The last glimmer of wanton eye,
Created a single tune for deaf, enshrined ear.

What vision of splendor stood before this near corpse?
Was it hope that bit as it sang its glad song?
I followed its melody,
No destination had I;
Song and dance of freedom helped me find home.

IT BROKE MY HEART

Everyone thought of your family highly,
Good neighbors right next door.
If only your closed door were opened,
What shock would fill the air.
On the outside,
For the world around you to see,
Your life looked happy and healthy,
Honored tribute to Mom and Dad.

"What a smart man is he;
A community beacon is she," say they.
"You are very fortunate
To have parents like them."
If the damage done you
Had been known to praise givers,
The only monument offered
Would be that of a concrete cell.

You tried to tell me,
More times than you really could,
Of the nightmare hell
You were daily living - not dreaming.
Each time you came,
It ended the same:
My name, a choked mumble,
Tear - streaked face, then hasty exit.

Verses From Above

Years later, I learned
From a most reliable source
What your charade
Of unspoken prose had purported.
Most of your childhood years
Had been ones of molestation;
Although your mother knew,
She said you were to blame.
When you ran away, Dear Child,
No idea had I the cause;
It broke my heart when the truth
I later discovered.
You sensed a kindred spirit
In one you tried to trust;
It broke my heart to know
You walked that road alone.

In reality, you (and all who are abused)
Were not alone at all.
For God Above was by your side,
Feeling all your pain;
He grieved for you
Then brought you through it all.
Now, you may use your pain for gain
By helping hurting others.

Judy A. Dees

JAD: Many students in my (almost) 25 years of teaching tried to tell me or give me hints of abuse they were suffering. They knew (although I didn't yet) that I would understand. Of the different types of abuse, sex abuse is considered the most devastating and the most damaging to the human soul. If you have been sexually abused (three degrees of sex abuse), KNOW that your life has been affected by it. Good news! God can make the crooked straight and the uneven even. He can restore what the locusts (of destruction) took away.

Verses From Above

FAKE ONE

Hey, You,
Fake one walking down the street!
Pretty smiles, friendly wave -
Both become you very well.
Unfortunately, they leave you
The moment no one is watching.

You whine, complain,
Then bite off your family's heads.
Those nearest you
Could just as well be dirt;
Your laughs and jokes
Become hisses and growls.

Someone must have convinced you
That you were rotten to the core;
Maybe you were
Verbally beaten or physically used.
Are you afraid others will see
The person you think you are?

Daily, you don your mask
Of niceness and civility.
What's sad is that you
Could really be, for all to see,
This nice, fake person
You try so hard to be.

Judy A. Dees

JAD: Are you the same person at home that you are in public? For the most part, I am now, but most of my life I had a face of many masks. I really don't think I knew who I was. Now, I know who I am and who I am in Christ. Each of us is fearfully and wonderfully made - and loved perfectly and greatly by the God who made us. He knows us totally and loves us, still.

SOFT, SPLENDOR MOMENT

When, in one soft, splendor moment
Hungry feelings isolated have been awakened,
Something inside released to suppress
The magic that moment was intended to bring.

Why not a natural response to pleasure afford,
But, instead, overwhelmed rushes of guilt and remorse?
Think not it be a reminder of innocent youth,
When the flower plucked then was much off nature's course?

Though plucked, this flower superficially grew
Into, what others saw, a most beautiful bouquet;
Inside the stem and rose petal face
No one could see a most delicate decay.

By God's saving grace, she still lives today,
But the truth of her past still wakes in her heart;
Her longing to share one soft, splendor moment
Leaves her still gazing at the wall of her mind.

JAD: Abuse victims often have intimacy issues. Ones who have been sexually abused by one or ones close in the family, have familial-tie issues; it is difficult for them, after marriage, to enjoy physical union. Previous to marriage, it might not have been a difficult issue.

DARE TO BE

Hanging framed on my walls for many a year
For all to see before spirits had sunk:
"I know I'm somebody,
'Cause God don't make no junk!"

That is something I want you to remember,
Children and students dear, when one lone night or day,
Deep down inside a despairing heart
All seems lost to doom, gloom, or decay.

That you came into being was no coincidence!
Each one of you, made in a special way,
Could only be fashioned from the
Master Potter's unique pattern of clay.

People will come and go in your everyday life.
Do they see the person you were created to be
Or a fake, copied in images of myriad others?
I dare you to be you - as I dare me to be me.

(P.S. I dare you to read Psalm 40:1 - 13!)

IT'S TIME

For such a time as this
Have I been called,
Wondering, waiting, knowing
Some tasks for me would come;
Never dreaming what my Lord Above
Had on His mighty mind,
Yet, somehow realizing it must involve
The love of my life.

You, Dear Teen,
Are more precious than gold,
But, too often, you've been treated
Like throw-away tin;
You, Dear Youth,
Our nation's most precious resource,
Have been cast away and abused
Like any old clump of dirt.

It's time to reclaim
That which has slipped away:
Your goodness and vitality,
Your value and worth;
It's time to repair
That which has been broken:
Your integrity and self respect,
Your heart and self worth.

I believe in my heart that all these poems are saying (for you or me):

(1) In any trouble (minor or major), take Jesus' hand, and He will carry you through. Imagine that, in the river of life, there will be shallow and deep water, holes of water, and roaring water. You may fall into each of them, but if you have a hand to pull you out, you won't be swept away or pulled under.

(2) No matter what sinful man (parents, siblings, employers, friends, strangers) says to or about you, GOD SAYS that you are fearfully and wonderfully made and that He loves you and will never, ever leave you or forsake you, even when your parents might. You are a unique creation made by His hand, and no one else in all creation is like you. You are His child, and once you accept Jesus as Savior and Lord of your life, no one can snatch you out of His hands.

(3) The most important decision you will make in your life is the decision to follow - or not follow - Jesus. That decision will lead to eternity in Heaven or Hell.

(4) Each person is in need of a Savior. All have sinned and fallen short of the glory of God - some worse than others! No matter how "good" you are, your goodness is as filthy rags to perfect God, so you need a Savior - Jesus Christ. No matter how "bad" you are, you can be washed as clean as snow and start your life anew. When you confess with your mouth to the Lord that you are a sinner and need His saving grace, then decide to turn from your sinful ways and make Jesus Lord of your life, you are forgiven. Your sins are cast away as far as the east is from the west. It is for the sick and sinful that Jesus died on the Cross at Calvary.

VISIT BRANSON, MISSOURI

When you come to Branson, MO (one of the nation's top tourist destinations), please be sure to visit Historic Downtown Branson. Branson began as a thriving logging community and is now an entertainment mecca, but HDB, established in 1888, is the heart of Branson and still resembles its roots with brick facades, Victorian lamp posts , and about 80 "mom and pop" shops and cafes. Visit our unique, historic area and come in to say hello to our friends and us: (These and more!)

Mr. B's Ice Cream & Deli (us)
The Fudge Shop
Branson Café
Rosa's Lost Treasure Chest
Branson Bill's Emporium
Jigglin George's Too Gifts Galore
Dick's 5 & 10 / Historic Owen's Theater
Clocker's Café / The Shack Cafe
Downtown Casual Wear & Western Wear
Thai Thai Cuisine / Branson Hot Hits Theater
Pinky Dink's Cupcakes / The Nativity Museum
Arkansas Diamond Mine
Ivy Rose Quilts /Ozark Quilts
It's Magic Jokes & Novelties
Old Fashion Candy Store
American Wear T Shirt Shop
Main Street Flea Market /The Classy Flea Market
Reish Shoe Store / Plum Bazaar
Smack's Deli & Ice Cream / Henry's Warehouse

Judy A. Dees

Elegant Illusions Created Gems
House of 1000 Clocks / The Flagstore
Mr. G's Chicago Style Pizza
Chappy Mall / Farmhouse Restaurant
Western Home Décor / Debi's Hallmark Gifts
Kay T Bugs Collectables
Ruby Lena's Tea Room / Rocky's Italian Eatery
Ozark Mt. Nut & Fruit / Burlington Annex
Lighthouse Gallery / Twice Born Christian Gifts & Books
Bee Discount / Patricia's Victorian House
Lil Shoppe of Leather / Sonya's Leather
Simply Barbara / If The Shoe Fits
Palate Fine Wine / Waterfront Trading Company
Crane Creations / Lightining Pawn
Locksmith's Salon / Chick's Barber Shop